T0208512

THE HOW-TO BOOK FOR
STUDENTS OF PSYCHOANALYSIS
AND PSYCHOTHERAPY

THE HOW-TO BOOK
FOR STUDENTS
OF PSYCHOANALYSIS
AND PSYCHOTHERAPY

Sheldon Bach

Routledge
Taylor & Francis Group

LONDON AND NEW YORK

First published 2011 by Karnac Books Ltd.

Published 2018 by Routledge
2 Park Square, Milton Park, Abingdon, Oxon OX14 4RN
711 Third Avenue, New York, NY 10017, USA

*Routledge is an imprint of the Taylor & Francis Group,
an informa business*

British Library Cataloguing in Publication Data

A C.I.P. for this book is available from the British Library

ISBN-13: 9781855758872 (pbk)

Typeset by Vikatan Publishing Solutions (P) Ltd., Chennai, India

For Rebecca, Matthew, and Julia,
who continue to learn and to teach me

CONTENTS

ACKNOWLEDGEMENTS

This little book began with questions from students, so I want to thank all my students at the New York University Post-doctoral Program in Psychoanalysis and Psychotherapy, at the Institute for Psychoanalytic Training and Research, at the New York Freudian Society and elsewhere for their abiding curiosity, their sometimes fierce discussions and their genuine help and encouragement. It is an honour and a joy to teach them and it continually revitalizes my hopes for the future.

Many friends and colleagues have read at least sections of the manuscript and made very useful suggestions, including Lew Aron, Jennifer Cantor, Jay Frankel, Richard Gottlieb, Robert Grossmark, Susan Roane, Doris Silverman, Aaron Thaler and Allan Waltzman. As always, my peer group, consisting of Steve Ellman, Norbert Freedman, Mark Grunes, and the late lamented Irving Steingart has been of immense help, not only in their direct reading of the manuscript but also in the ambiance of free discussion and inter-penetration that we have created together over these many decades.

I am grateful to my patients who have taught me almost all that is contained in this book and made many suggestions for improving my work, including the one who suggested that referring to patients as "difficult" revealed my biased perspective and that instead I might learn to think of them as challenging.

I cannot say how grateful I am to my family who have supported me throughout the years, to Rebecca and Matthew and Julia, and, especially, to my wife Phyllis Beren who has lived this with me, tolerated my discouragements, and edited the manuscript with her exceptional insight and common sense.

I wanted to add my appreciation for my publisher, Oliver Rathbone, who was willing to take a chance on something outside the box, and to Lucy Shirley and Kate Pearce who so ably fulfilled their duties as publishing assistant, project manager, and hand holders.

ABOUT THE AUTHOR

Sheldon Bach, Ph.D., is Adjunct Clinical Professor of Psychology at the New York University Postdoctoral Program in Psychoanalysis, a Training and Supervising Analyst at the New York Freudian Society, and a Fellow of the Institute for Psychoanalytic Training and Research and of the International Psychoanalytical Association. He is in private practice in New York City.

INTRODUCTION

When I first became a student of psychoanalysis in the 1950s I used to keep Edward Glover's *Lectures on Technique in Psycho-Analysis* by the side of my bed, as if I hoped to absorb through osmosis the absolute confidence that he exuded about matters psychoanalytic. Years later, when it no longer mattered, I learned that he had written his lectures only a few years after graduating from analytic training, at a time when his experience would have allowed him to know not much more than I did. Were I to say that this has taught me a lesson, it might not be entirely accurate.

For it seems essential in life to idealize people and principles, and equally essential to temper or modify our idealizations through the test of reality. Some things that I have learned from teachers have been priceless beyond saying, while others were shibboleths that took me many years to shed.

This is a book that grew out of the many practical questions that my students have asked me over the years and that I tried to answer with little explications that I distributed to the class. While I do believe that there is ample hard evidence for the usefulness of psychoanalysis and psychotherapy (e.g., Shedler, 2010), this little book is neither an evidence-based compendium nor an attempt to summarize general practice or the viewpoints of others, but is simply my own current personal opinions. They should thus be approached with caution, for they are offered only as one person's take on complex and often debatable subjects. I have tried to be honest about what I do, but am fully aware that my opinions may sometimes represent a minority in the field, perhaps even a minority of one. In the end, we all have to make our own decisions about how we practise, within the broad constraints of formal legal and ethical principles, but sometimes people are not terribly forthcoming about what they actually do, and this can be confusing to beginners in the field.

At some point I realized that I could never live long enough to learn all the things I needed to know, and that I had to resign myself to doing many important things with a certain degree of ignorance and trying afterwards to repair the damage.

But I do believe that the future of psychoanalysis lies in recognizing that there are multiple truths and learning to live with them, and that this would be a good prescription both for our patients and for ourselves.

Because this is not a scholarly effort I have borrowed freely from the many analysts, living and dead, who have influenced me and given references only when I had a specific reading to recommend. I hope that the many whose work I have assimilated but not specifically mentioned will be tolerant of this first effort to sketch a simple manual without turning it into a scholarly compendium.

CHAPTER ONE

How to choose
a psychoanalytic theory

When I began in this field we all studied Freudian
theory because at that time anything else was
considered "not psychoanalytic". It was a difficult theory and I studied it assiduously with, among
others, David Rapaport, who seemed to believe that
you couldn't be a Freudian unless you learned chapter
seven of *The Interpretation of Dreams* by heart.

Nowadays there is a smorgasbord of theories available and beginners often are inducted into one or the
other almost by chance, depending on whom they happen upon as a supervisor or analyst. Fortunately, more
and more institutes are offering courses in orientations
other than their own, so that students are often faced
with a panoply of rich and varied viewpoints that can at
times seem quite confusing.

It took me a while to realize that major psychoanalytic theories have generally been constituted around
the personal character structure, culture, and world-
view of their originators, an unsurprising conclusion.
If that is the case, it would seem reasonable that you
might choose a theory as you choose a friend, that is,

primarily because of personal compatibility. In this sense you can become a personal friend of some of the greatest minds in our field such as Freud, Ferenczi, Klein, Winnicott, and so on.

As your clinical experience increases and you discover that your chosen theory does not seem to completely answer or even to deal with some of the clinical facts you encounter, you may find yourself reading within other theories to help you with specific problems. That is the best way to learn psychoanalytic theory for, as most people discover, technical and theoretical papers can seem almost meaningless until you actually have lived through the clinical experience necessary to understand them.

Thus your friendships change as your life experience matures, and although you may hold on to the oldest friendships out of some sense of loyalty, if they have not also grown along with you, then you may have a hard time feeling as comfortable with them as you did in the first flush of youthful enthusiasm. Such may also be the case with psychoanalytic theories, but since new and interesting versions are being born and reborn all the time we can, if we remain flexible, be assured of having enough friends to last a lifetime.

CHAPTER TWO

How to do an initial interview

In an initial interview the patient is seeking relief
from some kind of suffering. He wants to find out
what the matter is and what can be done about it.
He is hoping to find that you are the person who can
help him.

In an initial interview you are trying to figure out
whether you can help this person, whether you want
him as a patient and, if the answer to the first two
questions is positive, how you can get him to come
back.

You should always have in mind a bottom fee below
which you cannot afford to work. If the patient cannot
reasonably meet this fee or if you do not want to work
with him, then you should make a careful referral (see
14, How to Make a Careful Referral). Although everyone reacts poorly to being rejected, you should make
a real effort to help the patient allow you to make the
referral, because it will generally be to his own great
advantage as well as to yours.

Try to be totally natural with the patient as if he
were your friend, which he might eventually become.

Begin by asking him how you can help him or what brought him here. If he says that he was brought by a taxi, he is demonstrating a thought disorder but this should not dishearten you.

It has been my experience over the years that the standard diagnostic classifications we have all been taught are not very helpful for predicting whether a patient can use therapy or whether he can be helped or healed. Some patients who meet the diagnostic criteria for psychosis, bipolar disorder or major depression can be immensely helped and even transformed by psychoanalysis, whereas others with more benign diagnoses may prove intractable for many analysts.

Analysability does not reside within the patient: it is a function of a particular patient working with a particular analyst at a particular time, and so your reaction to the patient as well as the patient's reactions to you are crucial in determining whether the dyad has a high or low probability of succeeding. That being said, it is also very useful to obtain a history of the patient's previous therapeutic attempts, if any, and in particular a clear idea of why they failed or were abandoned. Nothing is more enlightening than to try to understand where the previous dyad failed, if we can leaven our critical judgment of the previous therapist with an appropriate remembrance of our own failures.

A history of previous therapeutic attempts is one small segment of the larger history of object relationships that, to my mind, is the most important information you can elicit in an initial interview. This history can give you a good sense of the patient's basic pathology, and also a sense of what kind of therapy is most appropriate, how long it is going to take, how difficult it will be, and how the transference might evolve. While every treatment is a voyage into the unknown, it helps to have some navigational aids even though they may turn out to be only partially correct.

There are, however, two major caveats about gathering information in an initial or even in subsequent interviews:

1. It is more important to conduct a psychoanalytic interview than to gather any facts at all, even such obvious facts as age or marital status. If you intend to treat the patient, then the worst possible kind of interview is the standard "psychiatric" kind of interview in which you are filling out a mental checklist. The patient, who may have trouble enough relating in an authentic manner, may then begin to feel that he is relating to a psychological machine, or that the facts of his life are more important than he himself. A better implicit message, particularly if you have hopes of treating him, is that you are totally at his disposal and listening without any particular judgment or expectation, either of reasonableness, coherence, or morality. This indirection is in fact the swiftest possible route to connection and healing.

2. Certain of the more challenging patients are completely unable to give a coherent, consecutive, narrative history of their life or even their recent past, and that is usually diagnostic. This should become immediately clear and it is then useless to try to obtain a history and may even be distressing to the patient who, like a brain-damaged person, may have a catastrophic reaction to this revelation of his incapacity. With such patients their past history does not yet psychically exist, and a large part of the treatment will be devoted to creating a mental space and a mental capacity that will allow past history to exist and to allow them to think in

the way that is necessary to construct a personal history (cf. Bion's (1962) *Beta Elements* and Freud's (1897) *Nachträglichkeit* (deferred actions)).

So in an initial interview along psychoanalytic lines, we are primarily trying to listen to the other person in order to recognize who he is, or at least to let him know that we would be available for this purpose should he so desire. Initially, not everyone wishes to be recognized and indeed, some have enlisted a multitude of defences against their need for recognition. Thus, for example, some insist that they are there to be instructed or to be told what to do, or for some other variety of quick fix; anything other than beginning a process of investigation whose duration and direction is unclear.

Depending on your readiness to work in individually adaptive ways, any place that the patient is willing to start at is good enough. Thus, for example, if the patient has come in crisis and seeks advice, I am perfectly willing to discuss apparently common sense solutions to problems, while still wondering analytically why he might need advice, reassurance, re-orientation, and so forth. That is, I am willing to do anything that will not compromise an ultimate analytic outcome allowing for transference analysis. Of course, analysts have differing views on what might compromise such an outcome, but that would take too long to discuss.

A final caveat that became clear for me while reading Ferenczi's (1995) wonderful *Clinical Diary*: do not accept cases or parameters and conditions that may cause you initial hesitation, unless you are absolutely clear about what you are doing. Although you may be tempted to overcome your initial doubtful feelings in order to be generous, to right a wrong done to the patient, or to show how much better you are than his previous therapists, you do so at your own risk. The danger is that as the transference engages over the years the parameters that initially caused you to hesitate may increase in emotional intensity until the countertransference endangers the treatment, which will be good neither for you nor for the patient. But of course this is one of the many perils of our profession that no amount of well-intentioned advice can entirely eliminate.

CHAPTER THREE

How to choose your personal psychoanalyst

It was more than 50 years ago that as a candidate in a doctoral psychology programme I heard a student ask the director how to choose a personal analyst. I remember his reply: "Take the analyst to a stable and see how the horses react to him." This was impractical advice even at that time, and more so now that there are no longer any stables in Manhattan. But the import was clear: training qualifications, reputation, and the number of books written were less important than some affective personal quality to which horses were more sensitive because their minds were presumably not distracted by cognitive considerations.

You should of course consider length of training and other qualifications, books and articles written, courses taught, etc. since these may sometimes indicate a depth of commitment, but do not be overly impressed by the accoutrements of reputation, since some highly reputed analysts, just as some highly acclaimed physicians, may be total duds.

Other things being equal, you should prefer an analyst who has practised a substantial number of hours per week, is readily available, and does not spend most of his time primarily involved with non-clinical work or travelling around the country. If you needed surgery you would choose a surgeon who has done the most operations. That being said, we have all learned much from people who were not full-time clinicians; you want a flexible analyst who is capable of learning from experience, and not one who just keeps repeating the same mistakes year after year.

Since many analysts get better with practice but also charge more, you should choose as experienced an analyst as you can afford. But it might be worth while getting a consultation with an analyst whom you think you can't afford, since you might learn something helpful, or he might be able to refer you to a respected colleague, or, if you have insurance, to look over your insurance provider list and make a recommendation. And there is always the chance that the two of you might be able to come to some arrangement after all.

The more you interview analysts, the more you will learn and the better choice you might make. This is difficult advice to follow since an initial interview can be quite nerve-wracking and a bad one may even be destructive. But this is one of the most important decisions you will make in your entire career and even life, so it is worth while doing whatever you can to make the best attempt to get it right.

Nonetheless, if you start an analysis and after a short time begin to have doubts about your choice, you should of course discuss it with your analyst and try to understand the transference implications. It is important at this point that you be totally frank about your feelings. But if you cannot do that or are still not resolved in your mind after talking it through you should say that you are thinking of getting a consultation.

No good analyst will discourage this, as most have been in situations like this before and understand that they are not omnipotent and should have nothing to hide. Get a consultant from a different source, and preferably someone who does not need the referral and who might be able to be objective. Search your soul, but have the courage of your own convictions.

Ideally, training analysts should be selected purely on their ability and experience as judged by their peers and, equally ideally, candidates should be able to choose analysts who are not members of their own institute so as to minimize power interests, competition, partisan cliques, and other conflicts that tend to interfere with analytic neutrality.

Unfortunately, we live in a less than ideal world and the narcissism of small differences has made it such that many institutes in North America still require analysis with an analyst from one's own institute. Also unfortunately, appointment as a training analyst has been (inevitably?) adulterated with political and other extraneous considerations so that the title does not at all guarantee that this particular analyst will be useful to you.

It is my personal opinion that a good analyst is someone who is at home in the interpersonal world, so that he can recognize reality and offer support, hope, and trust, and who can also be at home in the intrapsychic world, so that he can offer attunement, understanding, and interpretation. When, how, and where to combine and employ these two complementary aspects of analysis is an art that comes naturally to some, can be taught to others, and remains elusive to many.

Given the complications involved, it is sometimes helpful to get a consultation or a referral from the analyst of a friend who seems to have made good progress in treatment. But remember that an excellent analyst might also make a referral that can be poor or perhaps just not right for you. Finding the right analyst is as personal a matter as finding the right spouse or partner. In the end, to repeat, you must search your soul and have the courage of your own convictions. If it does not feel right and it cannot be talked through, it is always legitimate to get another opinion.

Clinical Illustration

Over the course of the years I have seen many people who have had analyses that did not work out as they had hoped or that ended downright badly. Those whose analyses ended well would of course not have appeared in my office. I have seen people who were sexually seduced or otherwise exploited by their analysts, and people who had breakdowns that were not resolved during the analysis: a breakdown that is resolved during analysis may have been necessary and is of course another story (cf. Winnicott, 1980; Thaler, 2010). I have also met people who were told by their analyst in the midst of the treatment that they were unanalysable. This last seems to me totally inadmissible, since the most that any analyst can legitimately say is that he himself is unable to analyse this patient. But to have your analyst imply that you are unanalysable or to hear it in the midst of the transference is both omnipotently high-handed on the part of the analyst and devastating to the patient.

All these patients needed immediate consultations to help them understand what had happened and to master the trauma, but hardly any of them got immediate consultations because, like abused children, they were too profoundly traumatized, ashamed, and self-blaming to once again seek help.

Thus it seems to me to be a psychological emergency if anything goes wrong in the course of an analysis, and this includes the illness and/or death of the analyst. While I believe that analysis can be quite extraordinarily helpful if it goes right or even partially right, I have now learned that it can be harmful should it go wrong, and I strongly advocate appropriate consultation when the situation warrants it. All of this should not discourage anyone from engaging in what most analysts have found to be an extraordinarily helpful, meaningful, and life-changing experience. Although costly in terms of money and time, it usually increases one's income and, above all, it continues to spiritually repay one's efforts throughout a lifetime.

CHAPTER FOUR

How to listen to a patient

When I was in training in the Fifties and early Sixties, we were taught to listen primarily for the unconscious meaning of what the patient was saying. Our ultimate goal was to convert the unconscious or primary process meanings back into conscious or rational thought. It was as if we were translating a foreign language, the language of dreams, back into everyday English. Some of us got to be quite good at this simultaneous translation, but it was never entirely clear whether it was the lifting of repressions that helped the patient, the fact that we were paying such close attention to them, or something else.

Of course this was a distortion of the kind of listening that Freud had sometimes recommended, which was listening without a defined goal, with free floating attention. That is still quite difficult to do, as getting paid to be purposeless requires an uncommon faith in the analytic process. It is still a lot easier for us to assume the role of translator, advisor, benign adversary, older sibling, eager relater, or whatever, especially since that often seems to be exactly what the patient would like us to do.

Although listening to the unconscious has gone somewhat out of fashion, it can still be quite useful to understand unconscious wishes, even if one may no longer always be so quick to interpret them. While for some patients understanding their unconscious may mean recognition and validation, for others it may feel like a blow to their narcissism or it may be perceived as a hostile attack.

Thus the way one listens and responds to a patient will vary from patient to patient and, indeed, from phase to phase in any analysis. Much of the time my goal is to listen or to say something in a way that will leave the patient feeling recognized, that is, feeling that the analyst really knows who he or she is (see *13, How to Understand the Need for Recognition*). If a patient can feel recognized and accepted for who he is, then the analysis is on track until the next phase when that feeling may possible diminish or disappear entirely. This feeling of being recognized is closely connected to basic trust (Erikson, 1963) or analytic trust (Ellman, S.J., 2007), which I believe is a cornerstone of the treatment.

For some patients in some phases, a feeling of being recognized may be fostered by interventions or correct interpretation, but for others these interventions may be perceived as impingements or narcissistic insults. This is where the analyst's experience, diagnostic acumen, and sensitivity come into play. Attentive listening is almost always safe, but the patient usually needs to hear in some way that we are alive and awake. This can take as little as a grunting noise or an occasional verbal underlining, but it may also require a spontaneous reaction that does not abruptly switch the spotlight from patient to analyst. All of this comes under the heading of empathy or attunement.

Winnicott (1969) also mentions that at times he intervenes just to let the patient know how wrong he can be or the limits of his own understanding. If one just listens in an attuned way, the patient, who may have rarely been listened to that closely, often begins to form an idealizing transference (see *10, How to Tell what the Transference Is*). Winnicott's somewhat blundering interventions, just as Balint's (1968) refusal of his patient's request for an emergency session, were designed to disabuse the patient of the notion that the analyst is omnipotent. In certain cases or at certain times in the treatment this may be a necessary thing to do. But at the beginning with certain patients, an idealizing/omnipotent transference can be of great value, because it attaches the patient to the treatment and may allow him to share an omnipotence and heightened self-esteem that he never knew before (Kohut, 1971). As usual, we arrive at "it all depends", and for this the only cure is one's personal experience or supervision. Even the most experienced of analysts will always benefit from collegial discussion, and working in a psychotic or near-psychotic transference absolutely necessitates such consultations.

Clinical Illustrations

1. A patient came for a consultation after her long-time analyst told her that she was stopping her practice. She told me the history of her life and then began a long angry tirade against her analyst, detailing how the analyst had made the wrong decisions on a number of fateful occasions that had led to adverse consequences for the patient.

   Towards the end of the hour she paused and, sensing something lacking in her affect, I said: "I think you are going to miss her terribly."

She burst into tears and then slowly began to talk about her loving feelings for her analyst and her fear of abandonment.

2. About two months into an analysis, a young man was describing to me the difficulty he had following directions while driving his car, and on inquiry he explained he had the same difficulty reading a map. I have often seen such difficulties in people who as children had been disoriented around their mothers, and this usually resolves as the analysis progresses and the patient begins to orient around the analyst. But there was something subtly different in this description and, remembering that he had once mentioned reading difficulties that he attributed to anxiety, I suddenly suspected that he might be struggling with some neurological deficit and wondered if he should see a neuro-psychologist.

The extensive testing revealed major psychomotor and visual difficulties that were successfully remediated by opthalmological interventions and neuromuscular retraining over the course of time. Later on in the analysis he began to show a more classic disorientation around the analyst's absence, which could then be analysed in the usual way.

CHAPTER FIVE

How to frame and change perspectives

Recently I was walking in High Line Park, newly built on an elevated rail track that runs over a part of the meat packing district in lower Manhattan. Suddenly I came upon a little amphitheatre in the air, two stories above the ground, with a huge picture window where the stage should be, looking down on Tenth Avenue. Now Tenth Avenue is a nondescript street, with few stores, few pedestrians, and uninteresting vehicular traffic. But framed in this huge window and from this aerial perspective, it took on an interest and meaning such that several dozen people were crammed into the amphitheatre, just staring out of the window at something that ordinarily would never have drawn their attention. My first thought was how wonderful it must be to be a creative architect!

But then I realized that analysts are in fact architects of the mind and that we are constantly engaged in framing, re-framing, and changing perspectives on our own and our patients' vision of things. For the way we see things, frame them, and give them perspective is essential to giving them meaning, and meaning is what makes life feel worth living.

I do not mean to suggest that we start by re-framing what the patient brings to us. Whether they are obviously paranoid, are severely depressed or have otherwise distorted what we take to be reality (and who knows what that is?), our first job is always to learn to see things the way the patient does, that is, to enter into their world, their frame, their perspective, and to live in it for a while. Without this we can never establish analytic trust (Ellman, 1998, 2007) and I believe that without analytic trust we can never really have an authentic psychoanalysis.

After some period of time, which may take from a few weeks to a few years, we can begin to allow our perspective to enter the conversation. But for those without much experience in the matter, I should mention that the insertion of the analyst's point of view may, for certain patients, provoke a potentially traumatic or catastrophic response that may even lead to unilateral termination. For others the initial negative response may be workable and eventually lead to trust and growth. With the most challenging of patients, narcissistic or psychotic, we may have to wait years before they surprise us one day by asking us for our perspective: "What do *you* think about this?" Before this, we have not really existed for them as a separate entity.

But even with such patients, their perspective is being subtly altered from the first day they are with us, simply because they have included us within their world, even if they only treat us as part of the furnishings. This mysterious process, known as psychic interpenetration or the interchange of affect states between patient and therapist, occurs largely at an unconscious level and is one of the main transformational engines of talking therapy. Psychoanalysts try to deal with this directly, under the heading of transference; other talking therapies may ignore it entirely but use it indirectly, since research seems to indicate that the success of any kind of talking therapy is highly correlated with patients' reports that the therapist was warm, related, and supportive.

But to return to the frame: framing is essentially a device for directing attention or, in the jargon that I learned in the Sixties, deploying attention cathexes. Analysts are taught to listen without a frame, with free-floating attention, or without memory or desire, until the patient's material begins to speak to us clearly, in its own unmistakable voice. Sometimes we might point out this voice, and at other times we might wait until the patient hears it for himself. In either case, we oscillate between trying to be frameless and trying to frame things, between paying no attention and paying extreme attention.

As I looked down through the window at Tenth Avenue, I realized that framing material in a particular way could give it a meaning that it had not possessed before. That was a visual frame, but a cognitive or emotional frame works in the same way. We ask a patient to pay no attention, to not frame and to free associate; but as the theme of the material comes into view, we frame it with a comment that brings the formerly disparate ideas or feelings into a meaningful relationship.

But there are many other kinds of frames as well: cognitive, emotional, spatial, temporal, perspectival, etc. Sometimes we try to enlarge the frame and sometimes to narrow it: if a patient is stuck in the past we might try to provide a present or envisage a future, not even necessarily by talking about it because, as we know, one cannot talk to a severely depressed person about his future, but often only by holding it psychically for them, or acting as if it really did exist. With other patients who are unable to make sense out of inner chaos or to focus on anything, we try to help them concentrate by recognizing the strenuousness of their efforts and believing in their ultimate success, in addition to analysing whatever motivation, conflicts, or defences we can explore.

If a patient is stuck in his mind, we try to include his body; if lost in his body, we try to include his mind. Thus we try for a holistic view of things so that, in the ever-changing constellation of people's waking and sleeping life, altered states of consciousness and chrono-biological rhythms, we help them to find once more the patterns that will bring a renewed sense of meaning to their lives.

CHAPTER SIX

How to recognize and understand self-states, alternate states, true and false selves, multiple identities, etc.

I think that the term self-state was popularized by Kohut (1971, 1977) and later used by the relational analysts, most prominently Bromberg (2009), as a way of organizing, speaking about, and structuralizing experiences concerning the self. From the Freudian perspective, "state of consciousness" is a related but more experience-distant concept, elucidated by Rapaport (1951) in his encyclopedic *Organization and Pathology of Thought*.

There seem to be multiple parameters to a state of consciousness, including certain patterns of affect, different kinds of body schemata, different organizations of time and of thought, and different degrees of awareness of self and other. Thus it involves self-feelings that include both mind and body; a total sense of one's self at a given moment in time. Everyone's sense of self or state of consciousness is changeable and changing: for example, awake or asleep, in drug states, meditative states, angry states, loving states, depressed states, exhilarated states, etc. But for some people these multiple states can all feel as if they are encompassed by or belong to the same person—one's self—whereas for others they feel as if they belong to separate selves or people or even multiple personalities. Thus there is a continuum along which people consistently feel as if they are more or less the same person, and also a continuum along which other people will regard them as being more or less the same person—the difference between "I don't feel like myself" and "He doesn't seem like himself".

Further complicating this picture are concepts such as Winnicott's (1965) True and False Self, which adds a continuum of self-states that range from those feeling spontaneous, authentic, and "true" or "real", to those that feel externally imposed, inauthentic, and "false" or "unreal". Inauthentic or false self-states seem correlated with massive external coercion or impingement—*you must behave this way even if it doesn't feel real to you*—whereas true self-states arise when the external environment, although inevitably coercive to some extent, nevertheless prioritizes spontaneous responses and facilitates their emergence.

It is not always so easy to distinguish between true and false selves since not only you the analyst but often the patient himself is not sure of the difference, cannot distinguish between them or has got it completely wrong. A start can be made if you try to be alert to what feels real, authentic, and spontaneous, both to you and to the patient. They may not always coincide.

Just last week a patient, who had been imprinted with a painful early attachment to a father who then disappeared, discovered that:

"It's as if I have a false self that everyone likes but it doesn't feel either real or genuine to me. It seems that if it's not painful, then it doesn't feel real or genuine. It's got to really hurt me in order to feel real …."

It helps to remember that experiences of extreme environmental impingement, such as brain washing, result in a total False Self and that lesser impingements fall on a continuum with the spontaneous True Self at the other extreme. While the False Self is generally part of our adaptation to the environment, it makes all the difference whether that adaptation was mainly forcibly coerced or mostly induced through love. Adaptations that have come about primarily through coercion may have to be undone again in analysis and reworked through love rather than coercion. This may entail the analyst having to put up with some rather uncivilized behaviour for quite a long time, until the patient spontaneously comes around (see *11, How to Deal with the Sadomasochistic Transference*).

Many years ago I pointed out that there are two kinds of consciousness that everyone shares, which I called subjective and objective self-awareness. In subjective awareness, we are lost in ourselves and oblivious to others, like in a daydream, whereas in objective self-awareness we are acutely aware of observing ourselves as if we were another person, sometimes to the extreme of feeling depersonalized. Compare in your mind the stereotype of an hysterical person who is walking through the streets lost in fantasy, with the stereotype of an obsessive who is walking through the same streets acutely aware of every movement of every limb and of the gaze of every onlooker.

But in fact we all oscillate between these two states of consciousness to a greater or lesser degree depending on what seems appropriate. It is conventionally inappropriate to be lost in your own fantasies while listening to a lecture, just as it might seem less functional to be acutely observing your own and your partner's every movement while making love. Many people have great difficulty either in finding the state of consciousness suitable to a particular situation, or else in shifting appropriately back and forth. Much has been written about the difficulty borderline patients have in achieving objective or reflective self-awareness, but that is only a small part of the larger issue of flexible shifting between states of consciousness or between multiple self-states.

We have generally thought of free association as useful in permitting unconscious material to rise into consciousness. But a related and perhaps equally important function is that "it facilitates the patient's learning to integrate and to shift flexibly among states of relatively objective self-awareness and reality adherence, and states of relatively subjective self-awareness and disregard of reality" (Rosegrant, 2005, p. 765).

Whether we are working with acute cases of bi-polar disorder or dissociative identity disorder, or with the more benign dissociations and multiple self-states, it is an important part of our therapeutic work to help our patients bring their opposing worlds of sleeping and waking and their various self-states and states of consciousness into a more coherent and meaningful integration.

By recognizing and accepting the patient's affects, body schema, thought organization, and self/other awareness, we "meet" his parameters through our attunement, enactments, and verbal interventions, and we bring him into a larger system of which the analyst forms a part. I believe that ultimately the analyst's attentive presence in this larger system does indeed lead to increased mutual trust and to mutual assimilation and interpenetration of affect in ways that have been described at length elsewhere. Sometimes this may happen without interpretive intervention, but I think that conscious formulation and symbolic understanding are the eventual goals of every complete psychoanalysis.

Many people are now writing about this systems aspect under the heading of the analytic "third", and an opening discussion may be found in *Psychoanalytic Quarterly* 73(1), 2004. Of the multitude of volumes that discuss how patient and analyst create a third, a handful of the many that appeal to me are: Aron (2001), *A Meeting of Minds*; Balint (1968), *The Basic Fault*; Beebe and Lachmann (2005), *Infant Research and Adult Treatment*; Ferro (2005), *Seeds of Illness; Seeds of Recovery*; Kohut (1971), *The Analysis of the Self*, and my own (2006), *Getting from Here to There*, as well as several works by Benjamin (1995, 2002), Ogden (1994), Pine (1990), and others. These range from Relational through Bionian, Kohutian, and Freudian but they all, along with so many others there is no room to mention, contribute some truth to an exceedingly complex and difficult task.

CHAPTER SEVEN

How to manage the telephone

Of my own three analysts, one never answered the telephone while he was with a patient (I was not even sure if there *was* a telephone in his office), and the two others always did. One of the answerers explained that he wanted to always be available for patients, but that he would get off the phone as quickly as possible and limit the number of calls to two per session.

Although the best analyst turned out to be one of the answerers, as a patient I was always at least slightly disturbed by this practice and have resolutely refused to answer the phone while with a patient except for emergency situations. Most of the time I even turn off the ringer, especially with certain people who are extremely sensitive to impingements, but sometimes I forget. This is part of my general policy of arranging the office, the lighting, the temperature, the pillows, etc. to suit each person's preferences whenever possible. I look back with horror at my early years of practice when, for example, I smoked without asking permission, although that was common practice at the time.

Although when I began in the 1950s few people would have dreamed of talking to patients over the telephone and, indeed, in some quarters having contacts with patients beyond the scheduled hours was considered a serious violation of parameters, nowadays most analysts do some work over the telephone within limits that each individually defines. Thus, some will freely do phone sessions whenever the patient is away or travelling or when the analyst is on vacation, whereas others may reluctantly do them only for special occasions. Some patients seem to welcome phone sessions because of convenience or because it easily plays into certain resistances and defences; others find that it helps them to speak about certain shame-ridden subjects they could never broach in person, whereas still others find it almost impossible to talk on the phone at all. Personally, I find it a very useful adjunct for some patients and I use it, along with email, for any patient who finds it helpful, especially in trying to maintain continuity over breaks, holidays, and with patients who travel frequently. Like any other parameter of the treatment, my hope is eventually to be able to understand and analyse the patient's use, non-use, or misuse of the parameter, as well as my own parallel reactions. But there is no one way or ways that are better than others; it a question of patient and therapist continually working on methods of communication with which they can both become comfortable.

CHAPTER EIGHT

How to get paid for your work

When supervisees have complained about difficulty in getting paid, or when I have had such problems myself, it has almost always been a question of the therapist's ambivalence about charging for services or lack thereof. Thus many people have difficulty charging when the patient does not show up, for whatever reason, or when the patient complains that they are not helping, or when they themselves feel that they are not helping.

One problem seems to be that it may not feel fair or appropriate to get paid for merely talking to someone, whereas it clearly feels appropriate to get paid for administering a psychotropic chemical to someone, even though it might be useless or even toxic. Now that brain studies have shown that talking therapy activates brain areas similar to psychotropic medication, we may yet come to accept that talking therapy can be as powerful a force as drug therapy for both help and harm.

It has taken me a long time to realize and then fully believe that the treatment begins when the transference is activated, sometimes even before the patient arrives at our office, and that it then continues unabated, during sessions and between sessions, on holidays and vacations, until the treatment is terminated and often for a very long time afterwards. From this point of view, I am being paid to recognize the transference and then to understand and manage it, whether or not the patient is physically present. Whether the patient or I believe that he is currently being helped or not being helped is also one part of that transference constellation.

When I first began to practise I did not feel ethically justified to charge for missed sessions, and it took a few years of experience with frivolous cancellations, seasonal influenzas, and the vicissitudes of defence before I came to the conclusion that I could not practise consistently well without an assured income. I now charge for all scheduled sessions when I am there except for national and religious holidays, and I make only very rare exceptions. I explain this policy very clearly as soon as the patient and I have agreed to work together. I have seen many therapists make all sorts of complicated arrangements such as: "You are allowed six uncharged cuts a year, plus one visit to your grandmother," and they have consistently caused ongoing difficulties for patients and therapist alike. So, while one solution may not necessarily fit everyone, it seems essential to somehow resolve in practice our complicated ambivalence about charging money in a helping profession. It may be of use to remember Winnicott's reminder that ending the hour promptly and charging fees are two ways of expressing our normal aggression towards patients.

When payment becomes an issue there may, of course, be important dynamic and resistance factors that will be unique for each case. But another more general factor is the patient's sense of who owns the treatment—to whom does the treatment belong? If the patient strongly feels that the treatment is yours, then each payment may be experienced as a sort of tribute, a narcissistic humiliation that at times may be more than he can bear.

If, on the other hand, the patient feels some share in the treatment, then payment becomes just something that has to be done to keep the enterprise going, less of a narcissistic humiliation and more of a mutual endeavour. It seems to me that whatever we can do to make the patient feel proprietorship in the analysis is something worth doing. This would include arranging the office environment to suit the patient's preferences, if possible (see 7, How to Manage the Telephone), scheduling flexibly, if possible, allowing open access to the waiting room, if possible, etc. Clearly no amount of flexibility in the real world can do more than scratch the surface, but they do allow us a little more leg room in dealing with deeply held unconscious convictions of entitlement or exploitation. Clearly some patients feel that they are not worth much, and others feel that we are in it only for the money, but Ferenczi (1995), who once reassured a patient that in case of loss of income he would see him for nothing, later regretted this decision and felt that he had made a serious mistake.

When I think that a fee needs adjustment, either upwards or downwards, I try never to be arbitrary, to make fee setting part of the analysis and to work out something that is mutually satisfactory, going along with the patient if at all possible. Of course I have stories of patients being seen at reduced fees who casually mentioned buying a Picasso, but also stories of patients who were paying me more than they could really afford until some mundane detail brought this to my attention.

I have little useful to say about managed care, since my largely negative experience with insurers who repeatedly "lost" submissions, were apathetic about clinical urgencies, and behaved as if they were dealing with profits to the exclusion of people, has moved me to work with them as little as possible. I am lucky to be able to ask patients to pay me directly, after which I will submit insurance bills and forms, write letters, advocate with agents, and do whatever I reasonably can to support their reimbursement, but my fee will not be contingent on their repayment. Obviously, this limits my clientele, but I try to make up for this to some degree by reserving a certain number of hours at a very low fee.

I have known a good number of therapists who have found a niche within the managed care framework that seems comfortable for them. Since the typical policy often does not cover very much, they might offer an out of pocket fee that the patient could consider and that would assure their treatment beyond a few brief sessions. Some policies might reimburse for only one session but allow the patient to add on others. It is important for the patient to obtain all the facts, and if they then want to use someone from a panel to which the therapist does not belong, I have often volunteered to go over the providers with them or to put the provider names on a mailing list server to see if anyone has had experience with them. Meanwhile, we can engage in political action and support research in an effort to demonstrate that holistic health care, including mental health care, might be far more effective and considerably less expensive than the fragmented and politicized system that we in the USA now enjoy.

CHAPTER NINE

How to understand and manage the transference

Most analysts agree that understanding, managing, and interpreting the transference and countertransference is the most important but difficult part of any psychotherapy. This note cannot pretend to even introduce the subject, so a number of additional readings will be appended to it.

Although Freud "discovered" transference and at times realized its importance, it is strange how little he wrote about it, and how confusing or ambivalent some of these writings are. This trend continues to the present day, suggesting that the transference is not only very important, but also broader than originally conceived and somewhat mysterious in its workings.

Initially it was viewed as simply the displacement of feelings that pertained to an earlier object, such as the father, onto a later object, such as the analyst. It is still viewed by many in this simple, restrictive sense. But in 1914 Freud expanded this to include the notion of a transference neurosis that encompasses the entire treatment and complicates matters somewhat. In the full-blown transference neurosis (or transference psychosis, as sometimes occurs), childhood relationships are replayed with the analyst consciously in the centre, and almost everything else becomes emotionally secondary to this compelling drama. This allows for interpretations such as "What you are experiencing now is what it was like for you then" to feel utterly convincing, and it uncovers long-lost states and feelings that had been repressed by childhood amnesia. Anyone who has been either a patient or an analyst in such a situation is left with an incontrovertible faith in the analytic process.

But, in my experience, not every analysis produces such a full-blown transference neurosis and, while the transference is always present, we may often find ourselves dealing primarily with transference positions, such as paranoid-schizoid or depressive positions, or mirroring or idealizing transferences. If and how such positions evolve into each other and the transformations they undergo, is a subject for advanced discussion, but their evolution is clearly dependent on the nature of the analyst's interventions, which in turn depend on his theoretical stance. I am trying, if that is possible, to simply describe the phenomenology of some things that the beginner analyst may expect to encounter.

I should also mention that the transference manifests itself not only with the analyst, where it may be difficult to interpret, but also with family members, friends, and colleagues, where it may at first be easier to spot and talk about. It is, for example, usually easier for a patient to admit that he feels his boss despises him the way he felt his father did, than to admit the same about the analyst.

But if we stay with the original notion of displacement of feelings, this can occur in many forms. We will use anger as an example, but it works the same with any affect: love, guilt, shame, etc.

Displacement of affect: the patient can feel angry at you just as he felt angry at his father.

Reversal of affect: the patient can feel that you are angry at him, just as his father was angry at him.

These simple displacements are complicated by the use of projective identification, a term first employed by Melanie Klein. In projective identification, the patient first projects an unacceptable part of himself onto the therapist, thereby blurring the boundaries between himself and the other. Let us say, for example, that he projects an angry, unacceptable part of himself onto the therapist. He then begins to act in a way unconsciously designed to make the therapist feel, think, and act as if he, the therapist, actually were the angry person that the patient perceives him to be. Most therapists unconsciously succumb somewhat to this pressure and begin to find themselves having angry feelings, even if they did not have them before. This is a strange and uncanny sensation for those who are not yet accustomed to dealing with it, because they may feel as if they are being driven mad through managing the patient's madness, but it is a common transference process with many if not all patients.

Projective identification is handled somewhat differently by different schools of analysts, and by individuals within these schools. Some tend to deal with it as if they had been given a hot potato and they interpret the projection immediately in an effort to give back the unacceptable feelings and parts to the patient. This works very well with some patients but becomes problematic with others. In an effort to deal with this, some therapists try to hold the angry part of the patient in their feelings and eventually to metabolize it therapeutically and return it to the patient in small doses that the patient will be able to handle. This must always be mutually managed, since some patients obviously have much lower thresholds and tolerances than others.

There are many other possible variations, all complicated by countertransference on the analyst's part, which runs parallel to the patient's own transference. While all analysts feel the pressure of projective identifications, we must also deal with our own unresolved conflicts which are inevitably resurrected by our patients who, by common agreement, during the course of any analysis develop an uncanny knowledge of the analyst's major weak spots and character flaws. There is generally no hiding place in analytic "anonymity", and we must resign ourselves, even if we remain factually anonymous, to having our character revealed over time to any perceptive patient who takes the trouble to look. Thus the real relationship exists alongside and also pervades the transference relationship, in ways that are extremely complex and ambiguous and that defy easy generalizations.

Many analysts feel that both transference and countertransference on the analyst's part are unavoidable concomitants of the treatment, not to be circumvented or deplored but simply to be accepted, understood, and utilized in the service of the treatment.

Clinical Illustrations

1. Many years ago I was asked to do a public supervision of a case at a psychotherapy centre. As the therapist was presenting this troublesome case, she repeatedly declared that she did not believe in the existence of transference. Taken unawares, I did not contest her, although it seemed to me that what she was describing was a clear example of a sadomasochistic transference and countertransference (see *11, How to Deal with the Sadomasochistic*

Transference). But I tried to be as helpful to her as I could without mentioning the word or using the concept.

After the conference it turned out that we were going to the same destination and, as if by chance, we found our-selves in a taxi together. After some small talk she said: "You know, there is one thing about this patient that really puzzles me!"

I asked what that was. She said: "Well, she's a really intelligent woman, but she keeps coming in session after session asking me these really provocative questions in a whining voice. She keeps reminding me of my three-year-old daughter!"

"Oh!" I said, with what I hoped was a friendly smile. "That's what we call the transference regression!"

2. Long before I began analytic training, one of my first patients was the daughter of a hard-working, idealized father-doctor who had died prematurely of a heart attack. I did some brief psychotherapy with her which she found very helpful. Some years later I accidentally ran into her in the street, and she told me again how helpful the therapy had been and, with a big smile, that she was now engaged to be married. Then she looked at me with a worried expression and asked: "Are you still working such late hours as you did when I saw you?"

3. An experienced analyst came for a consultation about a patient he had been seeing for a few years. The patient presented with a severe borderline disorder: she was depressed and isolated, felt that life had no meaning, and was unable to complete the coursework for her degree. She spent most of her time playing computer games and dreaming of anonymous romantic encounters. After a few years of analysis she was able to finish school, get married, and find a good job in the fashion industry. The analyst felt that although her character had not changed much, she had made substantial progress in adaptation to real life.

This all collapsed when her husband became ill with a life-threatening disease. The patient fell into a depression once more, lost interest in her work and marriage, and felt that life had again lost all meaning. She adamantly refused to consider the analyst's suggestions that the husband's illness replicated events in her childhood when her mother had a post-partum depression after the birth of her younger brother and had been unable to function for quite a while.

The analyst tried to empathize with the patient's feelings, but when he again tried to make some interpretations about the patient's reactions to these events, the patient became more and more angry at him, cut down her sessions and kept yelling that his interpretations were useless and made things worse.

The patient then had several consultations with therapists recommended by her friends. She began to talk about leaving and eventually the analyst came to me for a consultation.

I tried to talk with him about the ways meaning is constructed developmentally, as the mother valorizes the child's spontaneous interests, actions, and productions. As I described this process, the analyst began to associate to things he remembered that the patient had told him: how when she came home from school even before her mother's depression she would try to tell her mother what had happened that day but that she showed no interest …; about how whenever she told her what was happening in her own life, the mother would interrupt with her own concerns … .

Eventually we both realized that the analyst was in some ways repeating in the transference exactly the thing the mother had done to the patient as a child—that he was not responding to the patient's actual experienced needs but that he was making interpretations, however valid, from his own framework just as the mother had done … .

He was taken aback by this but felt that it was true. He changed the way he thought about the case. He stayed more with the patient's feelings, stopped making interpretations and tried to validate the patient's bereft feelings and her valiant attempts at self-cure. The patient slowly began to respond, casually mentioned that she had stopped going on consultations, and her talk of leaving eventually dropped away … .

It took another two years before the patient could gain some perspective on the episode and see that the analyst's understanding had been "correct" but premature for where she was at the time.

CHAPTER TEN

How to tell what the transference is

One way of thinking about this extremely complex subject is to imagine that all analyses have at least two transferences running at the same time: one in the foreground and one in the background (Treurniet, 1993). The one transference, sometimes called primordial, basic, narcissistic, or background transference, is a transference to the analyst as the environmental mother, that is, to the analyst as primarily a function for holding and containing rather than as a person to be related to. This is the transference that keeps the analysis ongoing, as It provides some varying degree of basic or analytic trust that allows your patient to fulfil the minimal requirements of an analysis, namely, appearing from time to time, speaking occasionally and paying his bills. This basic transference is largely preconscious or unconscious and handled through management, although it may become an object for analytic examination early on if trust is lacking, or later on as the analysis proceeds.

The other type of transference, sometimes called classic, neurotic, object-related, Oedipal, or iconic transference, is to the analyst as a partial or whole object who is being related to in some psycho-dynamic way, on both conscious and unconscious levels.

If your patient is neurotic, has whole object relationships, a history of relatively deep, stable, or continuous relationships, and a relatively untraumatized background, or even a traumatized background that has been digested and can be talked about with reflective awareness, then he may be viewed as reasonably well attached and will form or seek to form a whole object neurotic transference that will generally play out multiple variations on Oedipal themes (a three person psychology) (see *1, How to Do an Initial Interview*). In this case the object transference will appear in the foreground, and the basic transference in the background, unobjectionable and unnoticed until some dynamic shift in analytic trust may thrust it strikingly into the foreground.

If, on the contrary, your patient is narcissistic, borderline, or chronically depressed and forms non-integrated self/other or part-object relationships, has a history of meagre, unstable, discontinuous, or shallow relationships and feels like a poorly attached child, then he will seek to form some variety of the basic, narcissistic, or primitive environmental transferences that Balint (1968), Winnicott (1963), and Kohut (1971) have described. This is his attempt at attachment to the analyst in the only way he can, in the way a child would attempt to attach. If it fails (often because of some countertransference interference), then he may regress or need to defensively employ a sadomasochistic transference, that is, move to a place where he experiences pain with the analyst or provokes him into painful retaliation as some attempt to remain attached, however ambivalently. This corresponds roughly to the varieties of poorly attached children (Slade, 2008).

If the patient is in the psychotic realm then he is usually too internally confused and overwhelmed, that is, fragmented, to form even a primitive idealizing or mirroring transference. Nevertheless, sadomasochistic dynamics may abound and the work consists in helping the fragmented parts or selves to survive and to coalesce to the point where a primitive type transference of the kind described above becomes possible.

In this schema every patient is potentially analysable, but the countertransference problems often may become more challenging as the levels become more primitively organized.

The normal countertransference in the primitive transferences is generally complementary to the prevailing transference and presents the following typical problems:

1. The patient's idealizing transference becomes too difficult for the analyst to hold, either because it becomes too disparate from the analyst's own self-image and arouses anxiety, or because it arouses shame about his own hidden grandiosity or inferiority. The analyst, in order to maintain his own narcissistic equilibrium, then intrudes with interpretations or actions into the idealizing transference and deflates it, leaving the patient feeling abandoned and angry: a repetition of the original trauma.

2. The patient's mirroring transference becomes too difficult for the analyst to hold and support, usually because the pull to continually mirror the patient makes the analyst feel left out, feel that he can't function as an analyst, feel he isn't necessary to

the process or even feel that he doesn't exist. In order to maintain his own narcissistic equilibrium, the analyst then intrudes himself into the mirroring transference with interpretations or actions and deflates it, leaving the patient feeling abandoned and angry: a repetition of the original trauma.

3. The patient's lifeless depressive transference may lead the analyst to give up all hope and to either detach his feelings or de-cathect the patient and emotionally abandon him, or else to attack him with interpretations in the hope of enlivening him. Emotional abandonment generally leads to the end of the treatment, whereas attack by interpretation generally leads to a regressive and defensive sadomasochistic transference.

Clinical Illustrations

1. An experienced analyst asks for a consultation because she finds herself getting unreasonably angry with her patient, a married woman with children, whom she has been seeing for a year and a half. The analyst's anger seems to revolve around her perception that the patient has not gone deeply into her problems, seems unwilling to listen seriously to her interpretations, and seems caught in a "childish dependency" towards the analyst even though the patient seems rather smart and competent in the out-side world.

When I ask how the patient feels about the treatment she says: "Oh, the patient feels fine. She says she's being helped very much and she thinks I'm just perfect and wonderful! That's why I'm puzzled that I feel so irritated with her."

When I ask for her view on the transference, she imagines that the patient is in a good maternal transference, although the patient had an angry and embattled relationship with her own mother who never seemed to like her.

I wondered whether the patient was trying to recreate this embattled relationship with her mother and, by projective identification, to get the analyst to dislike her too.

But I also wondered aloud with the analyst: if you were in a good mother transference, would you feel as if you were always being ignored or not treated as a person? This patient is treating you as if you were part of the furniture, even if it's good furniture.

As I explain the nature of the narcissistic transference and her role as a self-object, the analyst begins to understand that:

A. The patient does not yet have sufficient reflective awareness or symbolic distance to be able to understand or utilize her interpretations, and
B. The analyst herself has feelings about being disempowered of her interpretive functions, not recognized as a whole, other, separate human being, and being over-idealized in a way that she experiences as totally unrealistic.

This understanding helps her to become less angry with her patient and better able, in this opening phase of the treatment, to fulfil her role in the idealizing and mirroring transferences. She has also been alerted to the possibility that the patient will now, or in the future, try to recreate the negative relationship with her mother.

2. One of my analytic patients who was sitting up, which she did from time to time, was therefore watching me when I reached for my water bottle to take a drink. But the bottle top had not been tightly replaced and as I was drinking, water was dribbling onto my trousers and shirt and it took me a moment to notice this and correct it.

Meanwhile the patient turned her head away, and afterwards she said: "I saw what was happening and I could have said something, could have stopped it, but instead I looked away."

I suggested that she didn't want to see me making a fool of myself or being a loser. She said that was exactly right and we talked for a while about how this must have replicated so many events in her childhood, watching her parents screw things up and being unable to stop them, and eventually even feeling responsible for it. This led to an iconic memory when, as a child, she had scrawled a very dirty word on drawing paper, meanwhile predicting to her friend that her mother wouldn't even notice it. When she showed the drawing paper to her mother, the mother had distractedly responded: "Beautiful! So nice!" This only re-confirmed what the child already knew: that the mother couldn't deal with reality and that consequently she was unable to authentically recognize her daughter.

The next day the patient went back on the couch, partly because she did not want to continue to watch me screw up, partly out of identification with her mother, and for other reasons as well. After testing the waters I decided not to pursue this at the time because she seemed to need to keep me idealized, but much later we were able to talk about all of this retrospectively.

CHAPTER ELEVEN

How to deal with the sadomasochistic transference

I include sadomasochistic relationships in defining perversions because in my experience they always go together, and although you may not see many actual sexual perversions in your practice, I am certain that you see sadomasochistic relationships all the time. Now Freud and many early analysts did not seem to think that perversions were necessarily coupled with other pathology like disturbed object relations, but I have never seen an instance where they were not, although I am probably defining disturbed object relations much more widely than Freud did.

What Freud did get brilliantly right was the link between sadomasochism and the beating fantasy, which many people believe to be universal. The Novicks' (1987) data suggests that beating fantasies are a developmental fact for most people, but that in certain children the beating fantasy becomes a fixed fantasy or a pathological obsession and that these are the more challenging cases.

Following Freud (1919), the conscious fantasy is: a child is being beaten, which covers the unconscious fantasy: my father is beating me. As we shall see, the beating may also become transformed into a permanent sadomasochistic way of loving. People who have beating fantasies often provoke other people in such a way as to re-enact the fantasy and thereby bring misfortune upon themselves.

While the beating fantasy is the essence of the masochistic and perverse situation, my own clinical experience suggests that sometimes we may not arrive directly at that fantasy in the treatment situation even though we may be sure it is there. Thus actual therapeutic improvement is not always based on reaching and analysing the unconscious fantasy but rather on reconstructing and re-living in the transference the early developmental years in which that fantasy was formed.

Now what do the early developmental years look like in which the essential sadomasochistic fantasy is formed? Years ago I used to believe that that this was a rapprochement phenomenon that peaked around two years of age and that was known as "the terrible twos" because the child was so antagonistic to parental authority and either resisted in a passive masochistic way or fought back in a sadistic way at every opportunity. But under the influence of the recent decades of infant observation I have come to realize that while the "terrible twos" are the most visible part of the syndrome, this may often be a pathology of the mother-infant dyad that may start from day one and indeed, may be visible from the very beginning. What clues one in to this perverse situation is that the interaction between mother and infant is unpleasant, either for the mother or for the baby or, usually, for both. Obviously, this situation can arise because the infant is especially difficult, perhaps colicky, or the mother is especially depressed, upset, or not good enough, or the combination just does not work for any of a variety of reasons. In the typical situation this lack of attunement or misfit gets repeated throughout all the ensuing developmental stages and often, without treatment, gets repeated throughout the patient's life. Of course, sadomasochistic trends can start at any time in development but the most severe cases often do refer to the early dyad.

In the analytic situation, as might be expected, one of the basic signs of a sadomasochistic transference is that the therapist develops a countertransference which feels unpleasant and may manifest itself in boredom, anxiety, or dread at seeing the patient or even forgetting appointments. We would have to assume that the patient is having similar or complementary feelings, whether conscious or not.

While the generally ungratifying sadomasochistic transference repetition that I describe is the most usual and expected foreground transference with borderline patients, with certain higher level narcissistic patients one may enter directly into a predominantly "new object" transference where the analyst becomes, not a repetition figure for an older mis-attuned primary object, but in fact the newer, good-enough object that the patient has always been seeking. This is especially likely to occur when the patient has in fact actually encountered a good-enough object at some important time in his life. Starting out with such a good-enough "new" object transference in the foreground will of course not preclude a negative transference in the background and will never prevent occasional regressions to the earlier sadomasochistic relationship, but it does make the analysis easier on both patient and analyst. Of course, even with borderline patients, our hope is that eventually the mistrust and exploitation of the sadomasochistic transference will be replaced by some newly found trust and mutual respect in a "new object" transference.

Now it is clear that, in the most oversimplified way, the cure for perverse and sadomasochistic object relations lies in taking the original misfit in the mother-infant dyad and reworking it in the therapeutic dyad. Hopefully we will get a somewhat better fit and the patient will understand the cumulative trauma he suffered, what he contributed to and continues to contribute to its persistent recurrence, and the larger implications this has for his life. Just to run through some of the most common patterns we see in this constellation:

The patient with sadomasochistic object relations may often give a history of idealizations and disillusionments with objects, personal causes, and life-events. This may be coupled with difficulties in being consistent in real life and difficulties with self-constancy and object constancy. Many of these difficulties with constancy and consistency are traceable to a lack of constancy in the parents, who usually turn out to have treated their children with what the Furmans (1984) have labelled "intermittent de-cathexis", that is, either a total lack of attention or more often an intermittent withdrawal or loss of interest that is the more devastating because it is so inexplicable. These patients, who have so often felt unaccountably dropped, then develop a mistrust and fear of dependency that pervades all their relationships and makes the therapeutic relationship, in particular, doubly difficult.

In compensation for this basic distrust, they then develop either an idealized relationship with an Other who treats them sadistically and whom they masochistically endure, or else they idealize themselves and become the sadistic partner in a sadomasochistic couple.

In contradistinction to the whole-object Oedipal attachment themes of the neurotic patient, the poorly attached sadomasochistic patient presents with these main separation themes that I have described elsewhere (Bach, 1994):

Masochistic: do anything you want to me, torture and destroy me if you must, but never abandon me!

Sadistic: I can do anything I want to you, but you will never be able to leave me!

In either choice they lack the trust that is necessary to form a healthy couple where the power in the relationship is mutually shared along with the idealizations and disillusionments. Thus they either get into sticky relationships from which they cannot extricate themselves, or they remain in totally superficial relationships out of fear that if they ever really committed themselves, they would never again be able to separate.

Along the same lines, these patients are usually afraid to get too excited or too committed to anything, because they are certain that eventually their excitement will be punctured and they will be dropped, and that the more excited and attached they have become, the more it will hurt. Separation from the original painful relationship with the mother has been and continues to be a life-long problem for these patients, and in the course of the treatment the management of separation issues becomes once again of crucial importance.

In my experience, the most difficult aspect of treating these patients is managing one's own countertransference. Because these patients have become attached to a primary object through persistent painful interactions, they have become in effect addicted to pain, and they will consistently choose painful rather than pleasurable attachments and painful rather than pleasurable interactions, including the painful interactions with the therapist. This is part of their attachment to the Mother of Pain rather than to the Mother of Pleasure. Phenomenologically, if they feel pleasure or love it does not feel real or genuine, and they experience enormous anxiety because they are losing their only certain and familiar object, the Mother of Pain. Thus, in a paradoxical way, pain becomes reassuring and pleasure becomes frightening and aversive. Unfortunately the analyst, who becomes unavoidably caught up in this paradigm, finds himself becoming either an object of pain for the patient, which makes him feel sadistic, or a subject of pain inflicted by the patient, which makes him feel masochistic. Here the analyst feels caught like a fish in a net, and I believe that how he understands and manages these feelings will inescapably determine the outcome of the treatment.

CHAPTER TWELVE

How to manage narcissistic disequilibrium

I t was said of Rabbi Bunim, the Chassidic sage, that he always carried two notes, one in each pocket of his trousers. One note read: "The world was made entirely for you", while the other note said: "You are nothing but dust and ashes". Depending on whether his self-esteem was too high or too low, he would reach into one pocket or the other and read the appropriate note to help rebalance his narcissistic equilibrium. Whether consciously or unconsciously, we are all continuously engaged in rebalancing our narcissistic equilibrium and in helping our patients rebalance theirs, even if only by our steady presence.

For those lucky enough to have internalized a steady presence in childhood, this self-esteem regulatory process is automatic and usually requires no thought. For those who have not adequately internalized this regulatory process, and that includes psychotic, bi-polar, borderline, and many narcissistic patients, the treatment itself becomes the major regulating mechanism; and the frequency of sessions, their continuity, and the analyst's homeostatic responses all contribute to the development of self and mutual regulation (cf. Bach, 1998; Beebe & Lachmann, 2005; Ellman, 2002, 2009).

If we define trauma as anything that interferes with the normal development of the self-regulatory processes, then a trauma arises when a child confronts a new emotional experience, whether internal or external, that is not being adequately recognized, contained, or managed by the environmental mother. Thus when a child (or adult) feels anger, anxiety, or love and the mother (significant other) either does not recognize or disparages those feelings, a small trauma occurs which, if consistently repeated, can become a cumulative trauma of great import.

The parents, as well as siblings and peer groups, directly influence the child's self-esteem. Thus, for example, if a mother reprimands her child, it makes all the difference whether her attitude is: "You are essentially a good child who has done something bad", or "You are a bad child!". Children are exceptionally sensitive and dependent on their parents' emotions, and when things go wrong they tend to blame themselves even if the parent is abusing them. In this way they preserve their parent as an object of hope and take upon themselves the task of learning to change and accommodate.

The therapist, who often becomes an object *in loco parentis*, may find himself willy-nilly in the position of regulator, and while with neurotic patients this may be an important subject for analysis, with more disturbed patients who lack the capacity for self-regulation, some developmental steps must be lived through before that capacity is achieved (see *16, How to Manage Vacations, Weekends, Illnesses, No-Shows and other Disturbances of Continuity*). Of course this is putting it in too dichotomous a fashion, and mixed cases are commonly found in actual practice.

Experienced clinicians know, for example, that when a depressed patient complains that he and his achievements are worthless, it is useless and in fact contra-indicated to try to convince him that "reality" shows otherwise. He will only feel misunderstood and we would, in fact, be misunderstanding his deep feelings of loss that can only be addressed by empathy and careful attention to his current state in the here and now with us. Insistence on the "reality" of his achievements or worthiness would be a repetition of the trau-matic misrecognition or disparagement of his feelings that might have occurred in childhood.

So the role of the therapist as regulator is neither simple-minded nor easy to fulfil, and in principle it involves neither role-playing nor an Alexander (1946) type "corrective emotional experience" although, in successful cases, the patient does in fact end up with a better emotional experience than he had in the past.

Now, in the course of treatment, and especially if a sadomasochistic transference intensifies, it some-times happens that a zero-sum game develops. In this game the patient can only feel better at the expense of making the therapist feel bad or, in the countertrans-ference, the therapist can only recover his upset nar-cissistic balance by making the patient feel bad. The patient disposes of innumerable ways to make us feel bad about ourselves, from openly criticizing us and dis-paraging the treatment to covertly not getting better. We likewise dispose of innumerable ways to make the patient feel bad about himself, from blaming the lack of progress on his resistance to losing hope in the viabil-ity of the dyad. One might say that a most important thread in the treatment is this interplay between the patient's narcissistic disequilibrium and the analyst's narcissistic disequilibrium, which often replays in some ways the particular disequilibrium that each one may have experienced as children.

It seems very important for the analyst to be aware of how the patient is affecting his narcissistic equilibrium, and also to make sure that he is not retaliating in kind. Even if it becomes clear to the analyst that the patient is trying to undermine his narcissistic balance, it may be counter-productive to interpret this before the patient is able to use the interpretation and not simply to hear it as a blaming attack. In this respect I always try to remember Winnicott's principle that the traumatic factors must "enter the psychoanalytic material in the patient's own way, and within the patient's omnipotence" (1960, p. 585). This is to say that, while doing whatever is necessary to maintain our own narcissistic balance (and a consultation may sometimes help with this), we try not to engage the patient in a life or death struggle and to allow him sufficient transitional space so that he either comes to see what he is doing or else becomes able to use our interpretive help.

So this interpenetration of the patient's and the therapist's affective lives can have both negative and positive consequences. In negative transferences they can undermine each other's narcissistic balance, and in positive transferences they can reinforce each other's narcissistic balance. In the ordinary case, both kinds of interactions will be experienced and worked through in the course of a thorough analysis.

How to understand
the need for recognition

A recognition scene depicts that moment at which long lost or even presumably dead characters are suddenly recognized for who they are and found to be very much present and alive. Recognition scenes abound in *The Odyssey*, where the old nurse Eurycleia recognizes the disguised Ulysses by his scar, in the *New Testament* after the Resurrection of Jesus, and in Shakespeare where, for example, Pericles recognizes his daughter who was lost as an infant. Recognition scenes can also encompass the discovery of one's own identity or true self, or of someone else's identity or true nature. The moment of recognition always places the event in a new and larger context, so that what formerly seemed insignificant or meaningless suddenly becomes drenched and suffused with meaning and emotion.

I recently came across a beautiful description of the awakening of a young girl who, for the first time in her life feels recognized by an adult:

> There was very little conversation in my family. The children shrieked and the adults went about

their business just as they would have had they been alone. We ate our fill, somewhat frugally, we were not mistreated and our paupers' rags were clean and sturdily mended so that even if we were ashamed, at least we did not suffer from the cold. But we did not speak.

The revelation occurred when at the age of five, going to school for the first time, I was both astonished and frightened to hear a voice speaking to me and saying my name.

"Renee?" asked the voice, and I felt a friendly hand on mine.

This happened in the hallway where, for the first day of school, they had gathered the children, as it was raining outside.

"Renee?" I heard again the inflection of the voice above me, and felt the touch of the friendly hand—an incomprehensible language—still pressing lightly and tenderly on my arm.

I raised my head, an unusual, almost dizzying movement, and met a pair of eyes.

Renee. That meant me. For the first time someone was talking to me, saying my name. Where my parents habitually merely gestured or grunted, here was a woman with clear eyes and a smiling mouth standing before me, and she was finding her way to my heart, saying my name, entering with me into a closeness I had not previously known existed. I looked around me and saw a world that was suddenly filled with colors. In one painful flash I became aware of the rain falling outside, the windows streaked with water, the smell of damp clothing, the confinement of the hallway, the narrow passageway vibrating with the press of pupils, the shine of the coat racks with their copper hooks where the capes made of cheap cloth were hung close together, and the height of the ceiling which, to the eyes of a small child, was like that of the sky.

So, with my doleful eyes glued to hers, I clung to the woman who had just brought me into the world.

"Renee," said the voice again, "don't you want to take off your raincoat?"

And, holding me firmly so I would not fall, she removed my clothes with the agility of long experience.

We are mistaken to believe that our consciousness is awakened at the moment of our first birth—perhaps we do not know how to imagine any other living state. It may seem to us that we have always seen and felt and, armed with this belief, we identify our entry into the world as the decisive instant where consciousness is born. The fact that for five years a little girl called Renee, a perfectly operational machine of perception blessed with sight, hearing, smell, taste and touch, could have lived in a state of utter unawareness both of herself and of the universe, is proof if any were needed that such a hasty theory is wrong. For in order for consciousness to be aroused, it must have a name.

However, a combination of unfortunate circumstances would seem to confirm that no one had ever thought of giving me my name.

"You have such pretty eyes," added the teacher, and I knew intuitively that she was not lying, that at that moment my eyes were shining with all their beauty and, to reflect the miracle of my birth, were sparkling with a thousand small fires.

> I began to tremble and searched her eyes for the complicity that shared joy can bring.
>
> In her gentle, kindly gaze I saw nothing but compassion.
>
> In the moment where I had at last come to life, I was merely pitied."

> (Muriel Barbery, *The Elegance of the Hedgehog*, pp. 43–44)

In this sad and lovely description of a child coming to life through recognition by an adult, we have a paradigm for an important element of the analytic process. Everyone whose sense of self has not developed or has been clouded by trauma, cumulative trauma, or just the ordinary difficulties of life, is in some way searching to have his true self found, named, and recognized by an Other, in this case the analyst. This recognition involves conflicts and tensions between sameness and otherness, between dependence and independence and between construction and destruction of the Other. I cannot go into the vicissitudes here, but they have been beautifully described by Winnicott (1969), Benjamin (1990, 2002), and Schwaber (1992, 2007) among many others.

Thus, as analysts, we may sometimes find ourselves in the extraordinary position of being able to endow someone with life, if only we possess the awareness and the ability to do so. I must sadly confess that, like so many of the grown-ups that Renee must have encountered before she met this teacher, I have too often blundered past this opportunity out of ignorance, countertransference, or the sheer inability to raise myself out of my own concerns and to experience where the patient is coming from.

But the times that we succeed in truly recognizing the patient or are, perhaps, recognized by him, are moments of quiet or intense joy that can be the most important part of any analysis. There, momentarily, it can seem that two souls have touched in a way that can be remembered and can sustain hope for the rest of one's life.

CHAPTER FOURTEEN

How to make a careful referral

There are many reasons you may not be able to work with a patient whom you have seen in an initial interview. You may feel unable to work at a fee that the patient can realistically afford, you may not have the hours or the time that the patient needs, or you may simply not feel able to work well with this particular kind of patient. As realistic as the reason may be and as carefully as you may explain it, most people feel hurt and rejected, even though they may have been ambivalent about coming. I have found that it often helps to make a careful referral.

I begin by explaining why I feel that this is not the best situation for them, and then offering to help them find something that will feel just right. I say that I will think about what they've told me and then call them within a week with the name of another therapist. It will take that long because I want to give this some thought and because I have to phone people and find someone who is right for them and who has the appropriate fee and hours available. I do not want to give them just any old name.

I ask them to see this person once or twice and to try to bring up with them any negative or uneasy feelings they might have. I explain that they might have negative reactions to something that the analyst said or did, to the office environment, or to almost anything. It does not matter how justified this might be; what matters is how the therapist hears them and responds to their questioning, because this might be a good indication of their ability to work together. If after one or two tries they still feel that this person is not right for them, they should phone me and we will talk about what happened and I will try to re-think things and give them another name. I am committed to repeating this process as many times as it may take until they find someone with whom they feel comfortable. I will continue to be available for consultation until they feel thoroughly settled.

I do not charge for this service beyond the initial consultation fee, because I do not want them to feel pressured to make a hasty choice. But it has never taken more than three or four tries, and I have often received calls from patients telling me how helpful they found this process to be. It is also almost always an important learning experience for me.

CHAPTER FIFTEEN

How to refer a patient for medication

It is very difficult to know when to refer a patient for psychoactive medication because a good part of the data base for psycho-pharmacological research has been so distorted by the medico-pharmacological-advertising complex that reliable data is difficult to come by (see for example Marcia Angell, 2009). The best non-partisan data I have found suggests that most anti-depressants may perhaps be slightly more efficacious than placebo, but not significantly so, and that the frequent side effects, including depersonalization, render them of dubious clinical efficacy for many patients. Nevertheless, I have seen occasional patients who seem to have been helped by anti-depressants and others who feel that they have been helped, and I support this without hesitation if the patient desires them.

It should be mentioned that for many depressed patients, vigorous exercise, relaxation techniques, and supplements such as SAMe, St John's Wort and fish oil have been shown to be as effective or more effective than many psychotropic medications (Kirsch, 2010;

Whitaker, 2010). So this is the way that I personally prefer to try first, other things being equal. With regard to the common objection that supplements are not controlled, laboratory assays on OTC supplements as well as other important information can be found at ConsumerLab.com and other places. One may also consult a knowledgeable healthcare practitioner about a reliable source for supplements and dosing information.

Possibly there are sub-groups for whom one modality works better than another, but we are currently unable to specify these parameters. Medication also appears to increase the risk of suicide for some patients, possibly related to its depersonalizing effect, but again not entirely specifiably. In addition, Robert Whitaker (2010) suggests, in his thoroughly researched book *The Anatomy of an Epidemic*, that anti-depressant and anti-psychotic medications may actually interfere with the natural course of recovery and thus effectively promote recurrent depressions and psychotic breaks. These issues have yet to be adequately clarified, although the media, drug ads, and many in the psychiatric establishment make it appear as if medication were the obvious, evidence-based choice. I must admit that I was somewhat hesitant to publish these thoughts, but I discovered in reviewing references that this and considerably more has been boldly asserted long ago by a number of independent psychiatrists, for example James Gordon (2008) in his popular book on depression, *Unstuck.*

Unfortunately for the clinician, the decision is further obscured by legal considerations, although in the event of patient suicide, one might nowadays be equally well sued for having prescribed or advocated medication as for not having prescribed it. So this is a decision that must be made individually, with the patient's wishes taking precedence in almost every instance.

Certain manic, bipolar or schizophrenic patients seem to find medication enormously helpful, even life saving (cf. Saks, 2008), whereas others do not, or else do not wish to be helped in this way. There is a large psychoanalytic and psychiatric literature on the meanings of medication, compliance and non-compliance (e.g., Busch & Auchincloss, 1995), which I cannot go into here but whose implications are diverse. Many therapists turn to medication when the patient is very anxious or suffering from panic attacks. With anxious patients I personally prefer to work without medication, if both participants feel able to tolerate the anxiety, but ultimately this is a question to be decided by the patient without pressure from the analyst.

I can only mention the fascinating but still mystifying issue of placebos and unconscious experimenter bias (Brooks, 2009). Although the gold standard is to test drugs double-blind against placebos, we still understand surprisingly little about this. More than 40 years ago Schachter (1964) demonstrated quite conclusively that he could induce either hyper alert or soporific reactions in subjects, all of whom had been given adrenalin, but half of whom had been told they were being given a sleep medication. It seems quite clear that for a valid comparison to be made, the subject must feel that the placebo is doing something to his body and is not just inert, for otherwise the trial is not truly blinded. So the real gold standard would be to test against an active placebo, with experimenters who are not indebted to the pharmaceutical companies, and with long-term follow-up, but few trials fulfil these criteria. We have learned much in the passing years, but in many areas we are still very far from an adequate understanding.

I say this especially for beginners who often tend to feel that medicating patients is a more "scientific" or a better-validated procedure than talking with them. But a close look at the evidence has convinced me that this is decidedly not true.

If, however, medication is decided upon, then it is important, especially for non-medical therapists, to find the right prescriber. I have too often seen non-medical therapists refer a patient to a psychiatrist for medication only to find that either the treatment or the patient himself has been co-opted by the other therapist. It is crucially important to find a psychiatrist whom you are certain is friendly to your therapeutic endeavours and will confine his role to consultation and medication. An ongoing consultation with the medicating person is always advisable and can very often be extremely enlightening. But normally one is safest with either a psycho-pharmacologist or, better yet, a psychoanalytically oriented psychiatric friend.

Some patients arrive pre-medicated, and I make no attempt to interfere with this unless they are on some elaborate cocktail that is clearly doing more harm than good. I always try to keep myself well informed about everything the patient is ingesting, both prescribed and self-prescribed, without necessarily forcing a discussion on him. I try to remain unobtrusive about these matters, unless there seems to be a clear and imminent danger.

But to return to clinical considerations: I believe that the very best treatment for severe depression or acute psychosis is to see the patient every day and to make oneself completely available to him day and night. In those cases where I have been able to manage this, the acute phase has lasted a relatively short time, with or without medication.

But this is a very difficult thing to do and many therapists, myself included, often find themselves unable to do it, for good enough reasons, even though they might want to. The closest one can come to this is still the best, because acute patients live and breathe through the transference to the therapist, and keeping the transference connected and clear is their best hope for psychic and physical survival. Those who are interested in treating these very challenging patients in a primarily psychoanalytic way can follow the trail from Ferenczi's *Clinical Diary* through Balint, Winnicott, Searles, Bion, Ferro, and many others who have explored the way and broken a path for us. But there are a multitude of other methods for working with these patients, as well as many possible combinations, and every therapist must find the method that fits in with his own personality, life style, aspirations, and abilities. In a similar way, every patient would ideally find the therapist whose personality and methods of working coordinate and integrate best with his own capacities and desires.

CHAPTER SIXTEEN

How to manage vacations, weekends, illnesses, no-shows, and other disturbances of continuity

In the old days when analysts saw patients six days a week, they often referred to the "Monday crust", that is, the "resistances" and other disturbances that arose during the break and that "interfered" with the treatment. Although we may understand the meaning of these phenomena somewhat differently, in these days of once or twice a week therapy we are often much less sensitive to the phenomenon itself.

Thus I recently saw in consultation an analyst who had arrived a minute or two late for a session and apologized to the patient who graciously said it was nothing, but at the end of the week the patient announced that he was forced to cut back his hours for financial reasons. The analyst never made the connection between his "insignificant" tardiness and the patient's reaction, nor did the patient.

But I believe that every break in the continuity of the treatment, no matter how small, presses a button in the unconscious that is labelled *ABANDONMENT*, that is, some form of emotional abandonment. According to the logic of primary process, this is true no matter whether the break is initiated by the therapist or by the patient, and no matter how realistically "insignificant" it may appear to be.

Once the transference has been engaged, and in some cases this may happen from the very first phone call, this principle applies, which is why it may sometimes be crucial to respond to a first contact as quickly as possible. Of course, all this is particularly applicable to challenging patients for whom separation is usually a major issue, but I think it applies to some degree to all patients.

For challenging patients, breaks initiated by the analyst such as vacations, illnesses, and weekends are particularly difficult. These patients do not believe they are being held in the analyst's mind, or sometimes in anyone's mind, and their experience is often that the very continuity of their existence is being threatened. Thus they may complain of being depressed, tired, or not leaving the house; of being confused, bored, or falling apart or, conversely, they may frantically engage in activities such as Buddhist chanting, sex, sado-masochism, or desperate socializing in an effort to bolster their failing sense of self (Bach & Schwartz, 1972; Bach, 1998).

We must remember that humans are herd animals, that connection and belonging are essential for all of us, that many patients have never fully established their separateness or their capacity to be alone, and that this defect becomes exacerbated once again as the treatment and the transference deepen. When over the weekend break a challenging patient begins to feel that he is somehow falling apart, it does no good to reassure him on Monday that we were actually thinking about him.

I now believe that with these patients it is the analyst's responsibility to try to ensure continuity by whatever method is possible, and I use the telephone, cell phone, extra appointments, email, written letters, or whatever means are available to try to maintain the connection or to bridge any kind of break in continuity. That is, after all, no more than one might do for one's friends, and in my experience maintaining an attitude of availability about this very often pre-empts or dissolves the patient's need to contact you. If patients come to truly believe that you are available to them whenever they need you, then you have in fact become internalized and are no longer necessary in reality. This sometimes presents understandable difficulties for most therapists, and I can do no better than recommend the lovely papers by Evelyn Schwaber (1992, 2010).

It may seem strange to some to include no-shows in this section, but it follows logically from the unconscious reversibility of actions. I have had challenging patients who came, stood outside my door for half an hour without ringing and then left, all without my knowledge. Meanwhile I had been trying to reach them on the phone, or checking to see if the bell worked. We were usually engaged in some kind of re-enactment of previous times when they had been left out in the cold. I have learned from this and other experiences that in an engaged transference the patient is always with you, whether they show up in your office or not. I have learned that the treatment continues to go on in some way whether the patient is physically present or not, and I have also learned not to harass the patient about no-shows and not to feel guilty about taking payment for them. The most important thing is that continuity must be preserved in the mind of the analyst. If it continues to exist in the mind of the analyst through every vicissitude, then eventually it will also establish itself in the mind of the patient.

CHAPTER SEVENTEEN

How to think about analytic process

M any decades ago when I was teaching a course in psychology, I asked the students to pair up and then to gaze uninterruptedly into each other's eyes for several minutes. This proved to be enormously intriguing for some students and impossibly difficult for others, and all of us were surprised at the extremes of emotion that it provoked.

I am reminded of this every time I begin seeing a new patient, for it seems that we are inherently programmed to connect to each other or to struggle against that connection, just as we have learned that an infant is programmed in many modalities to connect to its primary caretaker.

In a similar way, I feel that whenever a patient walks into our office an analytic process is potentially engaged, and that this process takes on a life and a shape of its own. And that is why whenever I do an initial interview (see *2, How to Do an Initial Interview*) I am concerned to evaluate the patient's potential for engaging this process, and also concerned that I do nothing traumatic, e.g., a quiz type "psychiatric" interview, that might potentially disturb, interrupt, or possibly abort this attachment process.

This process, which begins from the first phone call even before we have met the patient face to face, will quite naturally assume a shape that we eventually label as the transference, provided that the analyst does nothing to interfere with the process. This is easier said than done because, not being acquainted with the patient's particular sensitivities, it is all too easy to commit a sin of commission or of omission. It is usually best to be simple, honest, and natural, while at the same time taking our cues from the patient as to what it is that they need, expect, and hope for. Most disturbances of the budding attachment, relationship, or transference are disturbances that arise because the analyst experiences some narcissistic disequilibrium (Kohut, 1977; Ellman, 1998) that makes it impossible for him to adequately hold the patient's experience. The classic example is from Kohut, namely, the analyst who, when his young Catholic patient was forming a priestly idealizing transference to him, found it necessary to tell her that he wasn't Catholic. She had neither asked nor wanted to know, but being confronted with the analyst's "reality" pierced her fantasy, and it required a consultation to get the process back on track.

Thus a good analyst may often look as if he is doing very little or even nothing at all, but what he *is* doing that is extremely important is monitoring, facilitating, and not getting in the way of the unfolding analytic process.

If we succeed in doing this well enough, then a drama begins to unfold that is infinitely various and many coloured, a drama in which we are permitted and required to participate and that forms one of the major attractions for leading the analytic life. I have hinted at just a few of the many forms that this drama can take (see *10, How to Tell what the Transference Is*; *11, How to Deal with the Sadomasochistic Transference*, etc.), and our literature is filled with fascinating articles that deal with this subject, e.g., Brian Bird (1972). There are many professions in which one can try to engage people helpfully, but analysts are specially privileged in that they are able to enter and re-enter the magical domain of the transference and the analytic process over and over again in the course of their working life.

CHAPTER EIGHTEEN

How to maintain your physical health and mental equilibrium

An informal survey of a few dozen colleagues, each of whom has been practising psychoanalysis from 30 to 60 hours a week for decades, has provided me with the following information. One of them exercises by walking up the stairs of his apartment building while talking on his cell phone; another does 90 second wall-sits while reciting Shakespeare; several walk each day or play occasional games of tennis, while most of the rest engage in some more directed physical activity like going to the gym, running, or working out at home. The women analysts seem to be more gregarious and more sensible about exercise than the men, some of whom are either maniacal or else totally neglectful. One or two do nothing that could be even faintly construed as exercise. This seems surprising in a profession where remaining seated for long hours at a stretch, often under severe emotional tension, is the rule.

The professional hazards are well known: lower back trouble and burnout are common. For the former, many analysts try to move between sessions, do exercises, wall-sits, yoga, Pilates, tai chi, and other mental and physical disciplines that aid relaxation. The right kind of personal psychoanalysis that unifies and integrates both the mental and the physical can also be quite helpful.

As to burnout: many analysts try to become involved in the ongoing professional life of their institutes and/or professional organizations. One can either join committees to do the unpaid and generally unrecognized day-to-day work that keeps these organizations alive, one can aspire to powerful positions and assume a leadership role, or one can, usually after an initial foray, drop out of psychoanalytic communal life and go it alone. Each of these positions has its pros and cons, which I cannot go into here, and each may be appropriate for different people or for the same person at different times in his life.

But the fact remains that practising psychoanalysis or psychotherapy is a lonely and isolating profession. I believe that for one's own welfare and for the protection of one's patients each analyst must find a way to keep his human balance and not become too isolated, too grandiose, or too despondent and overly dependent on patients for feedback and gratification. This is not to deny the sometimes profound experience that working with patients can provide, but simply to emphasize the obvious point that some balance is necessary.

Most analysts obtain this balance through some combination of their personal life, hobbies, their professional organizational experiences, and some kind of self-organized experience such as peer groups, study groups, supervision, etc. As I have often emphasized, working with challenging patients who may be diagnosed as narcissistic, borderline, psychotic, or manic-depressive presents special difficulties and almost invariably demands that the analyst, no matter how experienced, find a compatible group, supervisor, or colleague to help him work through the unavoidable ongoing tensions and internal processes.

When I first began practising I was consciously disciplined about not staying out too late, drinking too much, or overindulging the night before work. In retrospect, with 50 years' more experience, this seems ridiculous, as I have occasionally done my best work when ill, exhausted, or otherwise *non compos mentis.* This is not to recommend inebriation or drug use, for most of the time it is really much better to be in good condition than not, but only to admit that there is no straight-line road to inspiration, intuition, attunement, and even clearly logical thinking.

Freud must have done some of his best work wreathed in clouds of cigar smoke, which can certainly put one into an altered state of consciousness. On the other hand, he adamantly refused sedatives and pain-killers throughout his years spent suffering with cancer, lest they destroy the clarity of his mind. So certain forms of altered consciousness seem to be propitious for doing psychoanalysis, whereas others may not be. This may vary dramatically from analyst to analyst.

If we take our lead from the writers and artists, perhaps I might quote this from Eckermann:

> "An air that was beneficial to Schiller acted on me like poison," Goethe said to Eckermann. "I called on him one day, and as I did not find him at home, I seated myself at his writing table to note down various matters. I had not been seated long before I felt a strange indisposition steal over me, which gradually increased, until at last I nearly fainted …. I discovered that a dreadful odour issued from a

drawer near me. When I opened it I found, to my astonishment, that it was full of rotten apples. I immediately went to the window and inhaled the fresh air, by which I was instantly restored. Meanwhile his wife came in, and told me that the drawer was always filled with rotten apples, because the scent was beneficial to Schiller, and he could not live or work without it ..." (1853, p. 289).

Most analysts have particular environmental conditions under which they work best; many women and some men have been known to knit while they work, and others doodle, play with their fingers, pick their noses, etc. Freedman et al. (1978, 1995, 1997) have done fascinating studies on the rhythmic inter-regulation between patient and therapist and studied the therapist's self-touching and self-soothing as part of an effort to self-regulate and re-synchronize with the patient when the material becomes too disturbing.

Many therapists seem to gravitate towards a particular state of mind that makes listening easier and more productive for them. Each may have their own particular way of achieving a transitional area, a balanced space between self and other. This psychological "porcupine distance", in which two people try to stay close enough to keep each other warm but not so close that they hurt each other, is part of our ongoing effort to maintain our psychic equilibrium in a situation that often threatens both our mental and physical stability.

CHAPTER NINETEEN

How to practise holistic healing

It was interesting to watch the reactions of colleagues when research first began to demonstrate that talking to people produced brain changes analogous to those produced by psychotropic medications. Even analysts who strongly believed in the power of talking therapy and the unity of the mind and body behaved with astonishment, as if some fairy tale had turned out to be literally true! Such is the difficulty we labour under in healing the split Cartesian world-view we have inherited.

But there may be more to this than mere cultural sluggishness or difficulty with metabolizing new ideas. Recent brain research suggests that minds and bodies, or the mental and the physical, are represented in different neural circuits, so that the phenomenological experience of body and mind is of separate categories, like numbers and colours. This might make it more understandable that we seem to cling to a Cartesian view even when we believe it to be incorrect, because it conforms more easily to the way the brain processes the world (Lieberman, 2009).

Even more difficult is the matter of applying our knowledge in the face of our patients' persistent question: how will talking about this help? This is a particularly difficult type of question for the beginner analyst, who may in fact be less convinced of the effectiveness of talk therapy than his more experienced colleagues. That is why it is so important for novice therapists to have the experience of doing long-term in-depth treatment. But the only sure cure for this comes when the beginner is persuaded by the efficacy of his own psychoanalysis, a condition that may take a long time to occur or, for some, may unfortunately never happen (see *3, How to Choose your Personal Psychoanalyst*).

The patient presents to us with an embodied mind, and it has often surprised and disconcerted me to see how many colleagues, both non-medical and medical, seem only too eager to leave the body to the physicians, an attitude reciprocated by the physicians who often, after a cursory prescription of psychotropics, seem only too eager to leave the mind to us. Thus, everyone sticks to the specialty in which he or she has been intensively trained and the patient is in danger of falling into a situation in which each part of his body is allocated to a different specialist. Interestingly, this resembles pathologies such as hysterical paralysis or phantom limb in which parts of the body are dissociated and have separate destinies, as well as pathologies such as multiple personality in which parts of the mind are dissociated (see: *6, How to Recognize and Understand Self-States, etc.*).

But the split between mind and body raises profound questions as well as practical issues for psychoanalysts. Clearly, the analyst must help to heal or to make whole, to bring together into a meaningful organic unity those parts of body and mind that have been dismembered and dissociated. But just as Western medicine so often treats conditions or diagnoses rather than the whole person, too often we analysts have conditions or diagnoses in the back of our mind as we deal with our patients.

Many great analysts have tried to explain where our mind should be as we work with patients, ranging from Freud's dictum on free-floating attention to Bion's famous advice to be without memory or desire. Perhaps one aspect they are all emphasizing is the holistic, that is, the attempt not to bring our own categories of perception, whether ontological, moral, diagnostic, or whatever to bear on the patient, but rather to allow his whole being to pervade our being until his voice makes itself heard. While this may sound mystical, and indeed it does have parallels from St John to Buber, in a less esoteric way it is also part of the everyday experience of good parents as they try to understand and to deal with their babies who are unable to talk. So this can certainly be learned, although it is not the only or necessarily the predominant approach that we take. If a patient comes in bleeding, or hungry, or clearly needing comforting, then we do what any decent person would do, as Freud and Fenichel did when they fed their patients. For balance is all, and a holistic view entails not only a balance between all factors affecting the patient, but also a recognition of the interdependence of these factors, as well as a recognition of our own place in the world and our own interdependence with our patients and with our environment.

REFERENCES

Alexander, F., French, T.M., Bacon, C.L., Benedek, T., Fuerst, R.A., Wilson, M., Grinker, R.R., Grotjahn, M., McFadyen Johnson, A., Vincent McLean, H. & Weiss, E. (1946). *Psychoanalytic Therapy, Principles and Application*. New York: The Ronald Press.

Angell, M. (2009). Drug companies & doctors: A story of corruption. *New York Review of Books, 56*(1), January 15.

Aron, L. (2001). *A Meeting of Minds: Mutuality in Psychoanalysis*. Hillsdale, NJ: Analytic Press.

Bach, S. (1994). *The Language of Perversion and the Language of Love*. Northvale, NJ: Jason Aronson.

Bach, S. (1998). On treating the difficult patient. In: Ellman, C.S., Grand, S., Silvan, M. & Ellman, S.J. (Eds.), *The Modern Freudians: Contemporary Psychoanalytic Technique* (pp. 185–196). Northvale, NJ: Jason Aronson.

Bach, S. (2006). *Getting from Here to There: Analytic Love, Analytic Process*. Hillsdale, NJ: Analytic Press.

Bach, S. & Schwartz, L. (1972). A dream of the Marquis de Sade. *Journal of the American Psychoanalytic Association, 20*: 451–475.

Balint, M. (1968). *The Basic Fault: Therapeutic Aspects of Regression* (pp. 170–171). London: Tavistock.

Barbery, M. (2008). *The Elegance of the Hedgehog.* New York: Europa Editions.

Beebe, B. & Lachmann, F. (2005). *Infant Research and Adult Treatment: Co-constructing Interactions.* London: Taylor & Francis.

Benjamin, J. (1990). An outline of inter-subjectivity: The development of recognition. *Psychoanalytic Psychology, 7S*: 33–46.

Benjamin, J. (1995). *Like Subjects, Love Objects: Essays on Recognition and Sexual Difference*. New Haven, CT: Yale University Press.

Benjamin, J. (2002). The rhythm of recognition: Comments on the work of Louis Sander. *Psychoanalytic Dialogues, 12*: 43–53.

Bion, W.R. (1962). *Learning from Experience*. London: Heinemann [reprinted London: Karnac, 1988].

Bird, B. (1972). Notes on transference: Universal phenomenon and hardest part of analysis. *Journal of the American Psychoanalytic Association, 20*: 267–301.

Bromberg, P. (2009). Truth, human relatedness, and the analytic process: An interpersonal/relational perspective. *International Journal of Psychoanalysis, 90*: 347–361.

Brooks, M. (2009). *13 Things that Don't Make Sense: The Most Baffling Scientific Mysteries of Our Time*. New York: Vintage.

Busch, F.N. & Auchincloss, E.L. (1995). The psychology of prescribing and taking medication. In: Schwartz, H., Bleiberg, E. & Weissman, S. (Eds.), *Psychodynamic Concepts in General Psychiatry* (pp. 401–416). Arlington, VA: American Psychiatric Press.

Ellman, S. (1998). Enactment, transference and analytic trust. In: Ellman, S. & Moskowitz, M. (Eds.), *Enactment* (pp. 183–204). Northvale, NJ: Jason Aronson.

Ellman, S.J. (2007). Analytic trust and transference love; healing ruptures and facilitating repair. *Psychoanalytic Inquiry, 27*: 246–263.

Ellman, S.J. (2009). *When Theories Touch: An Historical and Theoretical Integration of Psychoanalytic Thought.* London: Karnac.

Ellman, S. & Carsky, M. (2002). Symbolization and the development of interpretable transference. In: Lasky, R. (Ed.), *Symbolization and Desymbolization: Essays in Honor of Norbert Freedman* (pp. 280–305). London: Karnac.

Erikson, E.H. (1963). *Childhood and Society.* New York: Norton.

Ferenczi, S. (1995). *The Clinical Diary of Sandor Ferenczi.* DuPont, J. (Ed.), Balint, M. & Jackson, N.Z. (Trans.). Cambridge, MA: Harvard University Press.

Ferro, A. (2005). *Seeds of Illness, Seeds of Recovery: The Genesis of Suffering and the Role of Psychoanalysis.* Hove: Brunner-Routledge.

Freedman, N., Barroso, F., Bucci, W. & Grand, S. (1978). The bodily manifestations of listening. *Psychoanalysis and Contemporary Thought, 1*: 157–194.

Freedman, N. & Berzofsky, M. (1995). Shape of the communicated transference in difficult and not-so-difficult patients: Symbolized and desymbolized transference. *Psychoanalytic Psychology, 12*: 363–374.

Freud, S. (1897). Letter from Freud to Fliess, November 14, 1897. In: Masson, J.M. (Ed.), *The Complete Letters of Sigmund Freud to Wilhelm Fliess, 1887–1904* (pp. 278–282). Cambridge, MA: Harvard University Press.

Freud, S. (1919). A child is being beaten: a contribution to the study of sexual perversions. *S.E., 17*: 179–204.

Furman, R.A. & Furman, E. (1984). Intermittent decathexis—a type of parental dysfunction. *International Journal of Psychoanalysis, 65*: 423–424.

Glover, E. (1927–28). Lectures on technique in psychoanalysis. *International Journal of Psychoanalysis, 8*: 311–338; *8*: 486–520; *9*: 7–46; *9*: 181–218.

Goethe, J.W. (1883). *Conversations of Goethe with Eckermann, J.P. and Soret* (p. 289). J. Oxenford (Trans.). London: George Bell & Sons.

Gordon, J. (2008*). Unstuck*. New York: Penguin.

Kirsch, I. (2010). *The Emperor's New Drugs: Exploding the Antidepressant Myth*. New York: Basic.

Kohut, H. (1971). *The Analysis of the Self*. Chicago: University of Chicago Press.

Kohut, H. (1977). *The Restoration of the Self*. New York: International Universities Press.

Lieberman, M.D. (2009). What makes big ideas sticky? In: Brockman, M. (Ed.), *What's Next? Dispatches on the Future of Science*. New York: Vintage.

Novick, K.K. & Novick, J. (1987). The essence of masochism. *Psychoanalytic Study of the Child, 42*: 353–384. New York: International Universities Press.

Ogden, T.H. (1994). *Subjects of Analysis*. Northvale, NJ: Jason Aronson.

Pine, F. (1990). *Drive, Ego, Object and Self: A Synthesis for Clinical Work*. New York: Basic.

Rapaport, D. (1951). *Organization and pathology of thought: Selected sources*. New York: Columbia University Press.

Rosegrant, J. (2005). The therapeutic effects of the free-associative state of consciousness. *Psychoanalytic Quarterly, 74*: 737–766.

Saks, E.R. (2008). *The Center Cannot Hold: My Journey Through Madness*. New York: Hyperion.

Schachter, S. (1964). The interaction of cognitive and physiological determinants of emotional state. In: Berkowitz, L. (Ed.), Advances in Experimental Social Psychology (pp. 49–79). New York: Academic Press.

Schwaber, E. (1992). Countertransference: The analyst's retreat from the patient's vantage point. *International Journal of Psychoanalysis, 73*: 349–361.

Schwaber, E. (2007). The unending struggle to listen: Locating oneself within the other. In: Akhtar, S. (Ed.), *Listening to Others: Developmental and Clinical Aspects of Empathy and Attunement* (pp. 17–39). Lanham: MD: Jason Aronson/Rowman-Littlefield.

Searles, H.F. (1965). *Collected papers on schizophrenia and related subjects*. New York: International Universities Press.

Shedler, J. (2010). The efficacy of psychodynamic psychotherapy. *American Psychologist, 65*: 98–109.

Slade, A. (2008). The implications of attachment theory and research for adult psychotherapy: Research and clinical perspectives. In: Cassidy, J. & Shaver, P. (Eds.), *The Handbook of Attachment Theory, Research, and Clinical Applications* [second edition] (pp. 762–782). New York: Guilford.

Thaler, A. (in press). Breakdown and recovery in the analysis of a young woman. In: Druck, A.B. Ellman, C.S. Freedman, B. & Thaler, A. (Eds.), *Freudian Synthesis: Clinical Process in a New Generation*. London: Karnac.

Treuerneit, N. (1993). What is psychoanalysis now? *International Journal of Psychoanalysis, 74*: 873–891.

Whitaker, R. (2010). *Anatomy of an Epidemic: Magic Bullets, Psychiatric Drugs, and the Astonishing Rise of Mental Illness in America*. New York: Crown.

Winnicott, D.W. (1960). The theory of the parent-infant relationship. *International Journal of Psychoanalysis, 41*: 585–595.

Winnicott, D.W. (1963). Dependence in infant care, in child care, and in the psycho-analytic setting. *International Journal of Psychoanalysis, 44*: 339–344.

Winnicott, D.W. (1965). Ego distortion in terms of true and false self. In: *The Maturational Processes and the Facilitating Environment*. New York: International Universities Press.

Winnicott, D.W. (1969). The use of an Object. *International Journal of Psychoanalysis, 50*: 711–716.

Winnicott, D.W. (1980). Fear of breakdown: A clinical example. *International Journal of Psychoanalysis, 61*: 351–357.

Printed in the United States
by Baker & Taylor Publisher Services